LOCAL KNOWLEDGE SURF GUIDES

Presents

The Mainland Mexico Surf Guide

2012 Edition

The Journey Awaits

Published by Local Knowledge Publishing, L.L.C.
LocalKnowledgeSurfingGuides.com

ISBN 978-0-9839788-0-0

Table of Contents

1. Introduction

Local Knowledge Surf Guides provide you with the most accurate, complete, and up to date surf information available. The *Mainland Mexico Surf Guide* compiles years' worth of research, knowledge and experience by Mexican and foreign surfers alike into an easy to use travel guide. By choosing Local Knowledge Surf Guides you've made a wise decision that will save you time, money and make your travels in Mexico easy and streamlined.

At Local Knowledge Surf Guides we believe in presenting accurate and honest information without ruining the thrill of discovery. This book describes many well known, and lesser known surf spots in mainland Mexico in an easy to use format with additional information and maps pertinent to every region and break. This valuable information will help you score more quality surf sessions on some of the most beautiful, surf rich beaches in the world. From the crew here at Local Knowledge Surf Guides, we thank you for your support and urge you to stay stoked and keep exploring.

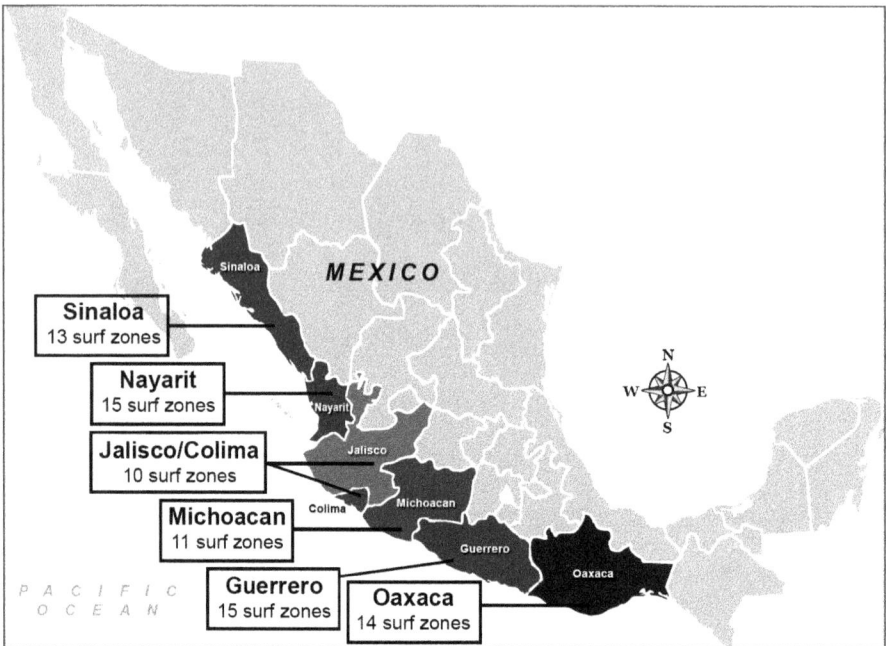

2. Mexico Surf Overview

The surf potential in Mexico is enormous. The mainland Pacific coast stretches for 1800 miles from the arid desert regions of Sinaloa in the north to the rich semi-tropical forests of Oaxaca in the south. The people of Mexico are as diverse as the landscape that makes up this beautiful country.

Mexico is open to nearly all Pacific Ocean groundswell. The best season for surfing in Mexico is April through November with consistent south swells. December through March sees less consistent swell from the south, however the northern half of mainland Mexico is open to large north and west swells that can produce world-class waves, although less frequently.

Sand-bottom point perfection - Photo C. Williams

In the past twenty years more people have come to Mexico to enjoy the warm weather, relatively cheap living and abundant waves. Some regions can get crowded in the high season. If you have a high threshold for adventure, know some Spanish, and have a copy of this book, you will find there are many high quality, less crowded waves to be had in mainland Mexico. Places like Sayulita, Puerto Escondido and Barra de la Cruz tend to attract heavy crowds, as they are easily accessible, high quality surfing destinations. In our opinion, it's the hidden gems between the well-known spots where you'll find the true Mexican surf experience.

Surfers from all parts of the world travel to Mexico to ride the world- class points and heavy, punishing beach breaks. Many locals in the prime surfing destinations make their living from tourism and exude a symbiotic vibe towards transient surfers. However, local attitudes and territorialism can be heavy in Puerto Escondido and the Salina Cruz region. For the most part Mexican surfers are welcoming, friendly and easygoing. Respect is usually given those who are respectful.

3. Climate

The climate along the Pacific Coast of Mexico is warm year round. Extremes in temperature are usually mitigated by the coastal marine influence. In the fall and winter months you can expect cooler evening temperatures (55-70F) and very pleasant daytime temperatures (70-80F). The summer is hot, but not unbearable. Daytime temperatures can get above 90F even by the coast.

The rainy season is late summer through early fall. During this time most of the coastal regions experience frequent rains, creating damp and humid conditions and occasionally mudslides and flooding. You'll likely be comfortable in board shorts and a t-shirt (or not) most of the time. If you're going for an extended period of time it's advisable to bring a long sleeve shirt and some light pants too.

4. What to Bring To Mexico

Adequate planning is the key to success for any trip. We believe in the saying, "It's better to have it and not need it, than to need it and not have it." If you take this in to consideration without over packing, you'll have a better time and spend more time surfing and less time stressing. The following suggestions will ensure you have a safe and fun time in Mexico.

☐ **Boards-** You can find just about any type of wave in Mexico but it's a good idea to have at least two boards; one that will perform well in heavy beach breaks and one that's more suited for softer points. If you have the room, bring a third backup board too. Be sure to bring extra leashes, fins, wax and a ding repair kit. If you are in a pinch, there are a decent number of used boards for sale in Pascaules, Sayulita and Puerto Escondido. New equipment is sparse and expensive, so come prepared.

☐ **Duct Tape-** You never know when you will need duct tape, but it always seems to come in handy.

☐ **Binoculars-** A decent cheap pair will do the trick. Access is limited in many places and being able to see a far off break will save you a lot of time.

☐ **Passport & Drivers License-** These are obviously imperative if you want to enter Mexico and drive yourself anywhere. We strongly advise making copies of these and all other relevant documents, laminating them and keeping them stashed somewhere safe. If you can, leave a copy of them with someone at home who can send them to you in case of an emergency.

☐ **First Aid Kit-** Get a good one, this is something you don't want to compromise on. It should have enough components to take care of any injuries you or others may encounter. Antihistamines are very important as the likelihood of having an allergic reaction to something is always amplified while traveling abroad.

☐ **Mosquito Repellant-** Unless you are opposed to DEET for health reasons, we suggest stocking up on bug repellant with

DEET in it before you go to Mexico. Bug spray is difficult to find in Mexico and you can never find the stuff with DEET south of the border.

☐ **Spanish/English Dictionary-** Unless you're fluent, this is a must-have. A travel size one costs only a few dollars and will save you in a pinch. It's always helpful to brush up on your Spanish before your trip.

☐ **Sunglasses and Hats-** Minimize your exposure to the sun, you will be in the water often enough. Give your skin a break when you're not.

☐ **Travel Insurance-** Travel insurance is a great idea no matter where you're headed, especially in Mexico. If you end up in a life threatening situation a good travel insurance policy will pay for a medical evacuation. Most likely you won't need it, but you'll be really glad you spent the extra money if you do. Most renters and homeowners insurance policies will insure your personal belongings while traveling. Call your insurance company to get the details. Most of the agencies don't readily advertise the fact that your personal effects are covered you while traveling, but if you ask specifically they will give you the details of the policy.

☐ **Sunscreen-** Stock up on sunscreen before you leave because it's very expensive in Mexico. It's also advisable to bring zinc oxide for your nose, ears and anywhere else you burn badly. The sun is very intense in Mexico and the last thing you need is blistering sunburn to set you back from surfing for days or weeks.

☐ **Wetsuit/Rashguard-** Depending on where you are in Mainland Mexico and the time of year, it may be a good idea to bring a spring suit. We have seen the water drop into the 60's in the fall/winter in southern Oaxaca. It's not uncommon for upwelling to cause a drastic decrease in water temperature overnight. If you're prepared, you'll be scoring a long session after everyone has gotten out.

☐ **Calling Cards/International Cell Phone-** If you can get an international calling plan in Mexico, go for it. If you are going to be there for a while, you can buy prepaid cell phones at many locations throughout Mexico through TELCEL. They are reasonably cheap and great to have in an emergency. Internet cafes are everywhere in Mexico, so set up a Skype account before you leave. It's a great way to make inexpensive international calls.

☐ **Maps-** Of course this book has maps of the relevant coastal surf zones, but it's very helpful to bring along additional road maps. Rough Guides makes a sturdy waterproof road map of Mexico. Check out www.roughguides.com for more information.

☐ **Prescription Drugs-** If you're bringing prescription drugs to Mexico, make sure you have them in the appropriate labeled bottles to avoid troubles if you get searched. Make sure you have an adequate supply. Refills are available in Mexico but likely won't be identical to what you get outside Mexico.

☐ **Tools/Parts-** If you're driving your own rig into Mexico, be sure to bring along enough basic tools to complete emergency repairs if needed. Hose clamps, radiator repair putty and extra fluids are lifesavers in a pinch. Before you depart, have a trusted mechanic look over your car and address any issues before you leave. Car repair and labor is considerably cheaper in Mexico, but we don't suggest holding off on a potentially serious repair in order to save some money.

5. Transportation in Mexico

There are many options for the traveling surfer in Mexico. The most important thing when planning your trip is to have an idea of how you want to get around in Mexico and pack accordingly, beforehand. If you decide to travel by bus and set out with too many possessions you'll find yourself overloaded and stressed out. If you have the option to drive through Mexico, you can take advantage of the extra space to pack cooking equipment and other supplies to stretch your travel budget as far as possible.

Traffic moves a bit slower in Mexico - Photo C. Williams

Whichever way you choose to go, be sure to plan ahead, read this book in its entirety, and make sure you've covered all your bases. It's always a good idea to make sure you have emergency contact information with you and adequate travel insurance before you go. The cost of insuring yourself is miniscule compared to the personal aggravation and expense incurred if something does go wrong.

Busses

Mexico has an excellent bus system that connects just about every major city. Bus stations are usually centrally located with easy to read schedules placed on the walls. If your Spanish is lacking, you can just tell the clerk where you want to go. Bus service ranges from economy to luxury. It may be a worthwhile to consider the length of your bus trip before deciding which level of comfort to go with. A long haul on a lousy bus can make for a miserable experience.

When traveling by bus, be aware of your surroundings and your possessions. If you are traveling with a friend make sure that one of you is awake at all times; bags and belongings have a funny way of disappearing while traveling by bus in Mexico. If you think you need to use the bathroom before a long bus ride, do it. Onboard facilities are often the last place you'll want to have to do your business.

Taxis and Colectivos

For local travel, taxis and colectivos are the way to go. Colectivos are usually small trucks outfitted with a canopy and benches in the back to accommodate eight or more riders in sardine-like manner. Don't expect much with the colectivos. They go slow, stop often and are usually crammed full with as many people as they can possibly hold. On the bright side, they are cheap and you'll get a chance to experience a popular mode of transport for many Mexicans.

Taxis are more insular so you won't have the opportunity to mingle with the locals quite as much. They cost more but can save you time if you're in a hurry. With both taxis and colectivos agree on a price and a destination before you depart to avoid disagreements later. Remember that most things in Mexico are negotiable and often drivers will quote tourists a considerably higher fare assuming that you'll be ignorant of the normal fare. If it sounds like too much, it probably is, and with some friendly haggling you'll probably be able to negotiate a better price.

6. Driving in Mexico

Driving through Mexico may be best option if you plan to stay for an extended period of time and want access to the most remote breaks. With driving comes the freedom to go where you choose at your leisure, however this is not without an added degree of stress and responsibility.

There are many rental cars available in Mexico. Usually you are better off going with a well-known international car rental company over an independent rental business. If you are on a slim budget you can rent beat up, older cars very cheaply in Mexico. Most of the time they are fine, but the old adage holds true - you get what you pay for. Regardless of where you rent, make sure you do a thorough inspection of the vehicle beforehand and note any dings or dents in the rental agreement. Rental car companies love to try and charge you for every little scratch.

Expect the unexpected while driving in Mexico- Photo C. Williams

Before you depart make sure your vehicle is in prime mechanical condition. Most American and Japanese cars are prevalent in Mexico and parts for repair are available. You don't want to take an Audi, Volvo, Mercedes, Saab or other atypical vehicle in to Mexico. You'll find parts nearly impossible to find and it will make your appear affluent and draw unwanted attention. The best car is one that runs perfectly, looks unattractive and doesn't draw attention. Consider having your windows tinted to make your car cooler and keep curious eyes from peeking in to see what goodies are inside your rig.

Road quality is poor in many areas but a 4x4 is not always necessary. The vast majority of spots are accessible in a 2WD vehicle. If you're traveling in the rainy season you may want to consider a 4x4 as some roads will be washed out. If you are on a budget go with a smaller 2WD and you'll save a lot of money on gas too.

The gasoline market in Mexico is monopolized by PEMEX, the national oil company. Stations are everywhere and usually provide adequate quality gasoline. If you get in a pinch in rural areas, you can find someone selling gas out of plastic jugs, however the quality is unknown and the price is double. To avoid this problem, we suggest never letting you tank get less than half full.

Your car insurance from the United States, Canada or elsewhere is almost always invalid in Mexico. Check with your insurance company beforehand and buy quality car insurance from a reputable agency. This is not an area where it pays to save a few dollars by going with cut-rate insurance. If you end up needing the insurance, you'll be glad you paid a slight premium for a comprehensive package from a reputable insurer.

The *couta* (toll roads) in Northern Mexico are generally in good condition and comparable to the U.S. interstate system. As of 2011 it costs about 2000 pesos in tolls to drive from Nogales to Tepic along Mex 15. This is an expense that many people who drive in to Mexico don't anticipate. Tollbooths are situated every 50-150 km and charge anywhere from 25 to 160 pesos each time. You have the option of driving along the *Libre* (free) roads, however they are much slower, more congested and poorly maintained. We don't suggest them.

Once you cross the border into Mexico you will be stopped at customs and have to register your vehicle for a fee of 38.00 USD if you plan to drive beyond the border region. Don't ignore this step. If you do, you'll be stopped by every official who notices you don't have your vehicle import sticker and will likely have to pay your way out of it each and every time!

South of Tepic Mex 15 ends and you begin coastal route Mex 200. This road continues all the way to Tapachula on the border of Guatemala. Mex 200 is a very curvy two-lane road that moves considerably slower than Mex 15. During and after the rainy season in the early fall, Mex 200 can become a tire devouring pothole minefield, testing the nerves of even the most seasoned drivers. Stay alert at all times and never drive at night!

Topes (speedbumps) are everywhere in Mexico. They are usually marked with a sign, but not always. If you hit one doing 80 km/h you will likely destroy your front-end suspension. Keep your eyes peeled and drive slowly.

Federale and military checkpoints are concentrated in the northern and southern border regions to intercept drug and weapon trafficking. With foreign license plates you can expect to be searched more often than not. Usually the officials will ask where you're from and where you are headed. It's best to remain calm and respectful to the *Federales*. Always address them with the formal *Senor*, even if it's 17-year-old soldier searching your car, which is not uncommon. Most times if they ask you to step out of the car, they will only take a quick glance at your possessions. You'll find the searches are cursory at best; their intention is to see how you react. If you have nothing to hide, you should be fine. We've been searched hundreds of times, but never for more than a few minutes. With that said, we can't advise strongly enough <u>not</u> to travel with drugs, guns, or other contraband in Mexico, it's not worth the risk of ending up in a Mexican prison.

Keep all your pertinent documents organized and ready to show officials upon request. Make copies of all your relevant documents and keep a set hidden in a safe place in the unlikely event you lose your primary copies. It's a good idea to leave copies with a close friend or family member at home in the event you need them mailed to you. If you take these extra measures, you will avoid headaches and have a great time.

7. Dealing with the Police

If you're considering traveling to Mexico, you've probably heard that police corruption exists. While this is true, the situation has improved drastically over the past 20 years. If you experience any corruption in Mexico, it will likely come in the form of a small bribe for a real, or fabricated traffic infraction.

There are three main police forces in Mexico that you should be aware of; the *Federales* (Federal Police), *Estatal* (State Police), and *Municipal* (Municipal Police). Generally speaking the Federales are the least corrupt and usually go by the book with tourists. The *Estatal* and *Policia Municipal* are the most likely to hassle you for a bribe. They are paid less and subject to less federal oversight. The good news is that if you know how to deal with them, you'll save time and money.

The Federales are your friends

If you get pulled over, say as little as possible. If you only speak a little Spanish you're better off pretending you speak even less. If they think you understand what they are saying it will make it easier for them to convey what they want from you. Be respectful but play dumb, it really works to your advantage.

Never outwardly offer a bribe to the police for a traffic infraction. This is viewed as an insult because it implies that you assume that they are corrupt and willing to take a bribe. Let them open the negotiations and go from there. If they try to exact a bribe they will likely tell you something along the lines of "I can give you a ticket, or you can give me the money and I will go pay the ticket for you." This is where a little careful finessing can save you some money.

Try to seem as broke as possible. The best thing you can do is keep some crumpled up bills in your car and act as though it's all you have. If they ask for 500 pesos and you scramble throughout your car to find 250 pesos worth of crumpled up 50's, 100's and 10 peso coins while telling them that's all you have they may get tired of dealing with you and settle for less than what was initially requested. Always keep your real cash stash hidden in you car while driving. The worst thing you can do is pull out your wallet to hand the officer your license and allow him to see a nice fresh stack of pesos in your wallet. If you remain calm and respectful they will likely let you go for a nominal fee or nothing at all. It's not uncommon to be let go with a warning and nothing else if you play your cards right. Keep in mind that most police officers are paid very poorly and have a hard and dangerous job. This is a situation where a little respect will get you further than being confrontational or dismissive.

8. Money Considerations

Cash is king in Mexico. Don't bother with travelers checks-they are not very useful south of the border. The best way to set up your finances for travel in Mexico is to establish a checking and savings account with your bank. Keep the majority of your money in the savings account and do online transfers to your checking account as needed. By doing so you will ensure that, in the off chance your ATM card is stolen, thieves will only be able to access what's in your checking account while your savings will be safe. ATM's and Internet café's are prevalent enough to make this system work well in mainland Mexico.

9. Health Considerations

Before you depart to Mexico, especially for extended stays, it is advisable to contact your health care provider to discuss precautionary measures. Malaria and Dengue fever are present in Mexico, especially in the southern regions and can ruin your surf trip. The CDC website covers all the relevant healthcare topics: http://wwwnc.cdc.gov/travel/destinations/mexico.aspx.

The old adage "don't drink the water in Mexico" remains true. As you'll see, all but the very poorest people in Mexico drink purified water. You can buy it in small quantities but your best bet is buying a 20-liter *garrafon,* which is a 20-liter plastic jug. They are a bit more cumbersome than small plastic bottles but they are much cheaper, and much more environmentally friendly. A 20-liter *garrafon* usually costs about 10 pesos. Make sure you get the screw cap variety; it's a lot easier to transport and store. Keep in mind the price is assuming you return the last one you used, so keep your empties to exchange!

Travel insurance is a great idea no matter where you're headed, especially in Mexico. If you end up in a life threatening situation a good travel insurance policy will pay for a medical evacuation. Most likely you won't need it, but you'll be really glad you spent the extra money if you do. Most renters and homeowners insurance policies will insure your personal belongings while traveling. Call your insurance company to get the details. Most of the agencies don't readily advertise the fact that your personal effects are covered you while traveling, but if you ask specifically they will give you the details of the policy.

The *Instituto Mexicano del Seguro Social* (IMSS) operates publicly funded hospitals throughout the country. They will treat anyone; however the lines can be unbelievably long. If you need medical attention for a non-life threatening issue, you're better off finding a private doctor or medical clinic. Most private clinics will see you immediately for 500 pesos or less. If your treatment involves injections or other invasive medical procedures, be sure to ask to see the syringe opened from the original plastic and verify that any surgical tools have been properly sterilized. In our experience, most doctors are quite good in Mexico and won't take offense to such a request.

10. How To Use The Guide

This guide is set up in an easy to use north to south fashion. The chapters are divided by state from Sinaloa in the north to Oaxaca in the south. At the beginning of each chapter there is a map listing all the relevant surf spots followed by in depth descriptions, other relevant information and directions to each spot.

Now let's hit the beaches.

SINALOA

Sinaloa is the first state in Mainland Mexico where there is real surf potential. Because of the shadowing from the Baja Peninsula, Sinaloa is almost exclusively a summer time surf destination. The varied coastline here has enormous surf potential with many high quality point breaks. Surfing here can be a waiting game at times because some south swells won't have enough power or the right angle to really produce in Sinaloa. If you're here in the summer, you can expect quality waves with reasonable consistency.

The landscape of Sinaloa is varied, starting as an arid desert in the north and transitioning to more fertile verdant setting in the south. If you're driving through Sinaloa, you can expect mostly smooth sailing; the roads are paved well and the landscape is mostly flat. Because tolls on Mex 15 are expensive and come up often, be prepared with enough pesos to get you through. They won't take a credit card. When driving through Mazatlan, don't be surprised when you're ambushed by an endless sea of people trying to wash your windshield at every stoplight. Clean or not they will wash your windshield, especially if you're a tourist. It's easier to tip them a few pesos and let them wash your windshield than try to wave them off because they won't listen.

Mazatlan is home to many quality points, reefs and beach breaks. Many surfers overlook Mazatlan, assuming that it's more of a tourist destination. The breaks here can get crowded, but it's usually manageable. Like most other places, if you show respect and wait your turn, you will likely be received well. Aside from the surf, Mazatlan is a cool town with a lot of nightlife and other non-surfing activities. Accommodations vary from cheap to extremely expensive. If you're working on a budget, you can usually find a reasonably priced room here, especially in the offseason. The great thing about staying in Mazatlan is walking proximity to many of the breaks. They are literally stacked on top of each other.

Further north of Mazatlan the small town of Dimas offers up some excellent point break opportunities. Dimas is much more isolated than Mazatlan. Accommodations are cheap and far less refined but the breaks are high quality. If you're going to Dimas, be sure there is a solid SW swell running or it may not be worth your time.

Celestinos

About 15 km north of Dimas at km 78 on Mex 15D is quality left hand point break. It's mostly a sand bottom point with varying conditions. If there is a swell, this spot almost always is producing. The wave itself is very fun and forgiving, overall an easy wave to surf. Generally, it's not crowded but there are almost always other surfers here if it's good. There are a few good options for camping here. Villa Celeste, Villa Tortugas and the Celestino RV park all usually have ample camping spaces and accommodations available for reasonable rates.

Patoles

About 5 km north of Dimas at km 69 off Mex 15D you pull off and head towards the coast. Patoles is a rocky headland point that can produce long epic lefts on a solid SW swell. Depending on how the sand is set up, there can be decent barrel sections on this wave. Patoles is very isolated, so bring what you will need for the day. You can stay in Dimas to the south, where most accommodations are very affordable. Local landowners may let you camp for a small fee if you ask. There is excellent seafood and fishing in this area too.

Dimas

There is a river mouth and beach break here that can produce quality waves. It's more fickle than Patoles or Celestinos and really depends on the sand setup, which is constantly changing. If it's small and the points in the area aren't really turning on, it's worth checking out Dimas.

Dimas as good as it gets

Marmol

About 35 km north of Mazatlan is the small town of Marmol. There is a long left hand point set up here that works well on a larger swell. It's generally a softer long point. It can be crowded here on the weekends, but the rides are long and there is usually a good rotation running if there is a solid swell. The deepwater canyon here seems to amplify the swell at this spot. Marmol is an easy daytrip from Mazatlan if you're tired of the crowds in town.

Cerritos/ Playa Bruja

About 8 km north of Valentinos is Playa Bruja. There is a good little point here that picks up swell and produces fun little rights and lefts. A bus runs up here from the center of Mazatlan. The wave itself isn't world class but definitely is worth checking out. Cerritos tends to be less crowded since it's outside of the downtown district.

Camarones

Just to the north of Valentinos there is a decent left point set up that can produce quality surf. It's not a perfect wave, but if you're in Mazatlan it can be worth checking out. Expect a crowd if it's on. There are tons of body boarders out here when it's working.

Valentinos

Valentinos is a decent right hand point wave right in the center of Mazatlan. Just look for Valentinos nightclub on the point, it looks like a castle and sticks out like a sore thumb. Valentinos needs a good SW swell to really turn on, but the wave can have some power if the swell and tide are right. Like all the breaks in Mazatlan, you can expect a crowd if it's working.

Los Pinos

This is a solid left hand point on the north end of the harbor entrance. When there is a solid swell running here, 150+ meter rides are not uncommon. The trick is getting a wave to yourself considering the crowds that this spot can attract. Los Pinos is definitely one of the longer points in the region.

Olas Altas

Just a few blocks south of Los Pinos is Olas Altas. It's considered the main surfing beach in Mazatlan. It's a beach break with a point on the south end that can light up if the swell is large enough. The beach break is fun and usually punchy here. Again you can expect to be sharing the waves with other surfers at Olas Altas.

Isla de Piedra (Stone Island)

This spot on the south side of the Port of Mazatlan is difficult to access. You'll have to drive south from Mazatlan and then head back north until you get to the Isla de Piedra community. From there you can head out the breakwater to the island where you will see the reeling right-hander. The wave itself is definitely one of the best in all of Sinaloa when it's working. It's a reeling barrel machine that rivals most any break in the region. If it's working, there will likely be a crowd here. Be very careful getting out to the break along the rock wall.

Barrons

There is an excellent sandbar left setup at the mouth of the Presidio River. Depending on the sand, this place can produce a reeling left that can go for a few hundred meters. This is a good option if you want to get out of Mazatlan for the day. It's usually best in the early morning before the wind starts to pick up. To access Barrons, go south from Mazatlan for about 15 km and then take a right on 17 towards the coast. Stay on 17 for about 10 km until the road hooks hard to the right. Stay straight on the road that heads out to the beach and you will be able to see the wave if it's breaking.

Playa Tambora

If you really want to get off the beaten path and roll the dice on a river mouth setup that can produce high quality waves, head to the town of Teacapan, on the border of Sinaloa and Nayarit. Heading south on Mex 15, take a right on Mex 1 in the town of Escuinapa. You will pass through a few small towns before the road ends in Teacapan. It takes about an hour to get out here from

Mex 15 and there are no guarantees that there will be a solid sandbar. The beach break here almost always has something worth surfing though. You will likely be surfing alone here. It's worth checking out if that's appealing to you.

NAYARIT

The lush and varied landscape of the Nayarit coastline is appropriately known as the Mexican Riviera. This section of coast offers many different surfing options. Due to its orientation, large southwest swells produce the best surf. Depending on where you are in Nayarit, even the largest of straight south swells can pass right by; the bottom line is the more west in the swell, the better for most spots in Nayarit.

Because of this region's proximity to Puerto Vallarta you can expect a slightly more refined experience. Tourism is a major part of the economy, attracting surfers and non-surfers from all over the world. Puerto Vallarta has become a haven for travelers looking for the most predictable and insular Mexican experience possible. If you're a surfer, you'll likely drive right past the high-rise hotels, souvenir shops and Hard Rock café unimpressed by it all. Aside from the random hurricane, Puerto Vallarta itself has very little to offer in terms of rideable surf. The good news is there are many international flights to Puerto Vallarta making it an easy access point to start your trip.

If you're going to surf in this region, we suggest staying in Sayulita, at least for a little while. This quaint hillside town situated on a small northwest facing bay is ideal in many ways. Although real estate investors have discovered it, it still retains a lot of its original charm. Accommodations here are a bit on the pricey side but if you look around, especially during the off-season, you can find a wonderful room for less than 400 pesos per night. There is also a trailer park in town where you can camp for much cheaper.

Sayulita is a great spot to set up home base if you want to surf the Punta Mita breaks, which are only 20 minutes away by car. If you head north, San Pancho and Chacala are easy day trips from Sayulita. Above all, Sayulita offers a nice environment with a healthy mix of travelers, tourists, surfers and locals with enough nightlife to keep you entertained once you're done surfing for the day.

San Blas

If you head north up Mex 200 and take a left in Las Varas on Carratera Federal 76 heading north, you'll find the sleepy fishing village of San Blas. There is a harbor mouth here with waves on both sides; the south end usually works better. Unless there is a very large SW swell, the waves here are usually on the smaller side. Depending on the sand it can still be a fun wave. Accommodations are very basic and cheap. Make sure that wherever you sleep, you have mosquito nets. The bugs in this area are unrelenting. If you like getting off the beaten track and exploring lesser-surfed areas, San Blas is worth checking out. Stoners Surf Camp at Playa El Borrego is where most traveling surfers on a limited budget choose to stay.

Empty San Blas left - Photo H. Blacket

La Puntilla

On the north end of the river in San Blas you'll find La Puntilla. When the sand is right you can find a fast and hollow left hand point. La Puntilla tends to work best on a good sized SW swell on a low-mid incoming tide. If it's working, 150+ meter rides are not uncommon here.

Stoners

Between San Blas and Las Islitas is Stoners. It's a right hand point that can really turn on depending on the swell. It needs a solid SW to work but it is easily the best wave in the area with the right swell. If you're coming from San Blas, you will need to cross the river and then hike to the break. You can drive to it if you come from the south. Again, the bugs in this area are unrelenting, so be prepared.

An average day at stoners- Photo C. Williams

Las Islitas/ Matanchen Bay

South from San Blas about ten minutes you will come to the headland of Las Islitas, where there is a right hand point that can hold a solid swell. Depending on the sand and the tide, this point can be very good. Just a short walk to the south there is a stretch of beach breaks that can produce if the swell isn't quite solid enough to light up the point.

Aticama

Another ten minutes south from Las Islitas is the small town of Aticama. On large south swells there is a left point here that can produce a decent wave. It is usually sectioned off, but if there is a swell running it can be worth a look. Aside from the surf, the seafood in the area is top quality and very cheap. There are plenty of locals who will be happy to cook you an excellent meal for a reasonable price.

Chacala (La Caleta)

About an hour north of Sayulita on Mex 200 you will come to the marked road heading towards the town of Chacala. If you end up in Las Varas, go back south about 2 km's and you'll see it. You will either need a serious 4x4 to get to the point from the town or you can hire a boat; there are plenty of fishermen happy to take you out there for a reasonable fee.

It's a long left point that really turns on with a substantial southwest swell; again the more west in the swell the better. Depending on the swell angle and the tide, this wave can have some juice behind it. Chacala can get crowded during the summer months. It's a roll of the dice; we have seen it pumping and nearly empty, and mediocre and packed; you'll be able to tell quickly once you get there.

San Pancho (San Francisco)

Ten minutes north of Sayulita you'll find the town of San Pancho. It's clearly marked along Mex 200 as San Francisco; San Pancho is what is what the locals call it. This quieter neighboring town to Sayulita has a long beach that's been known to hold some sandbars over the years. It can be great or it can be closed out shore break. Conditions depend on the season and how much sand the rivers have deposited lately. Occasionally there is a left off the south point but it really needs a substantial SW swell for that to work.

__Overview of Punta Mita Breaks__

The spots listed in this book are the best known and most surfed waves along Punta Mita, a phenomenal surf zone with lots of potential and relatively good accessibility. If you spend some time here and blaze your own trail when a swell is running, you will likely find other waves worth surfing. Bring some binoculars and befriend the locals. You may find a break to yourself.

Sayulita

There is a decent right hand cobblestone reef in Sayulita that produces soft rights on any swell SW to NW. This is a great spot for beginners; because of that there will be no shortage of tourists on rented foam boards learning to surf. There is really no need to compete for this wave since there are plenty of breaks in the region that offer surf better suited to intermediate and advanced surfers.

After the fall rains the river mouth a bit further up the beach can produce a decent left hander that's been known to barrel. The contents of the river can make the water quality rather poor though. Raw sewage can flush out the river after torrential rains. If it smells bad, consider the consequences of getting violently ill in a foreign country. It may not be worth it.

In the winter, Sayulita will pick up W and NW swells too. The reef will offer both rights and lefts and can produce a bit more size than on a south swell.

Patscauro

Just a few minutes west of Sayulita heading towards Punta Mita you'll find the small town of Patscauro. There are decent waves at this beach break but few traveling surfers surf here. There is a lot of surf tourism in this area and the locals like to keep some things to themselves. If you're feeling adventurous go check it out, but use your best judgment.

Punta Mita

Out at the end of the point is a right hand reef bottom point that can hold some sizeable swell. You can walk out there but it is very far and rocky. You will need shoes, patience and lots of water if you want to walk it. If you can get a group together, your best bet is to hire a boat for a few hours to take you out. You can find fisherman who will take you from Punta Mita, Sayulita or La Cruz de Huanacaxtle to the south. The best guys know the waves well and will likely know what is the best call for the day.

Punta Mita does best on a solid southwest swell. Be aware of the reef bottom, you don't want to hit it. If you get hurt, it will be a long walk or boat ride back. It is definitely one of the best points in the region when it's working.

La Lancha

South about two km's from Punta Mita is a small turnoff on the ocean side where you can park to surf La Lancha. It's a reef bottom setup that likes a medium to solid SW swell to really turn on. Rights and lefts peel from a central A-Frame with the rights usually holding a better shape and longer ride. Look for the cars parked here off the main road on the ocean side. It's best to stash your valuables elsewhere and leave your windows open with nothing available to steal since there will be no one there to watch your car while you surf.

Burros

Burros is definitely a regional classic. South from La Lancha another two km you'll see the Palladium hotel on your right. You can pull in here and drive down towards the gate and go left down the dirt road before the gate. Ask the guy at the gate to the hotel to keep an eye on your car and bring him a beer or two or some pesos and everything should be fine. Cars have been broken into here but a tip for the gatekeeper is cheap insurance.

If you go another one km south from the entrance to the Palladium you'll see an electricity transfer station on your left with a pull out on the right. Depending on the time of the year you can usually drive down that path on the right to the beach and park right in front of the break. If the path to the beach at the transfer station is passable, it's much more convenient than parking at the Palladium, plus you can keep an eye on your car.

A fun afternoon at Burros

The wave itself is a highly ripable, predominantly right hand reef break. On a good day it's similar to a B-quality Trestles. When it's on with a solid SW swell running, expect a crowd. You will find an array of different experience levels at Burros; find where you fit in and you'll get some waves. Burros is an excellent spot to practice roping cutbacks on its long walled up shoulders.

Pools

About one km south from Burros is a small point with a large house and a nice in ground pool and hot tub. There is a mediocre right hand point here that turns on occasionally but it's very shallow with many draining sections over uneven rocks. If you're a slab hunter who enjoys that kind of thing, this wave can be appealing, but be prepared to pull urchins out of your feet/back if you wipe out. On lower tides it's not worth it to try and surf this wave. The good news is that few people usually do, so you will likely have it to yourself.

Veneros

Southward down the beach another 2 km is Veneros. There is a public parking lot on the ocean side of the road with easy access to the beach. There is another right hand reef setup here that can produce decent surf on the right swell. To the south of this reef setup are a series of shallow sandbar beach breaks that can really produce on fragmented swells. If it's solid south, expect closeouts, but on a localized wind swell or other fragmented swells these sandbars can really light up producing peaky draining barrels.

JALISCO / COLIMA

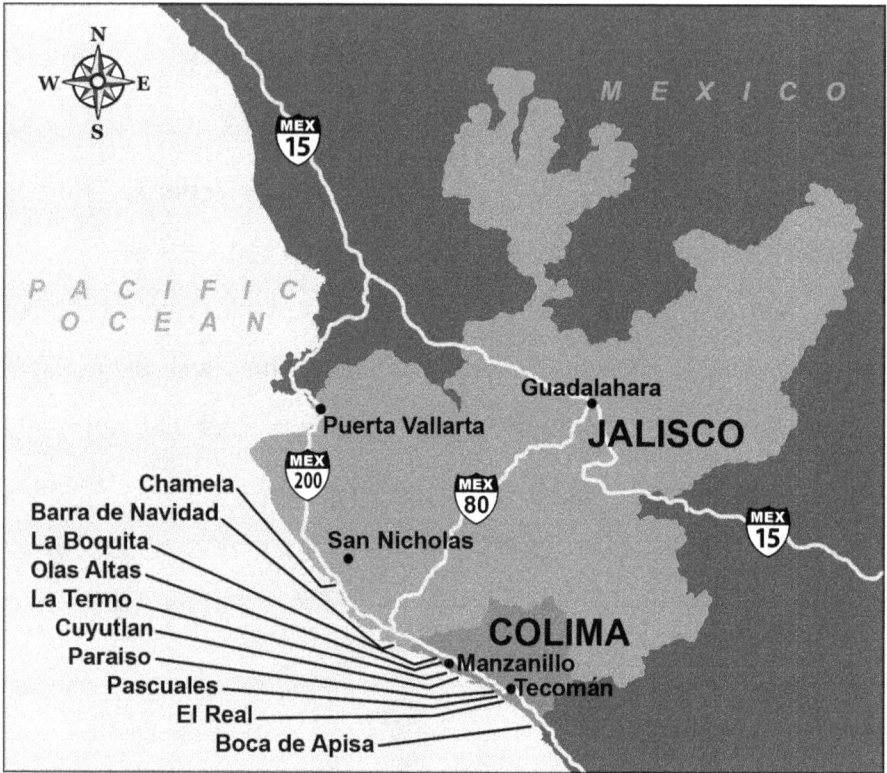

Jalisco is often overlooked as a major surf destination in Mexico because much of the northern section of the coast is inaccessible. The landscape and the people here are wonderful but there is little quality surf. On your drive south from Puerto Vallarta towards Manzanillo you will find tropical hillsides dotted with

Blue Agave (tequila) farms interspersed with rushing mountain rivers and waterfalls. Mex 200 bypasses this section of coast as it weaves through the mountains, leaving the inhabitants of the few coastal towns largely isolated until you get to Chamela.

This highly mountainous region on the northern coast is sparsely developed and the roads are terrible. This section of coast is mostly a waste of time if you're searching for waves unless you have nerves of steel, a bulletproof 4x4, and a thirst for the unknown.

The road from Puerto Vallarta to Manzanillo seems to wind endlessly and you rarely get above 70 km/h. Stock up in Puerto Vallarta before you leave, and make sure you have plenty of gas. Once you get into the mountains, there are no gas stations and you will be stuck having to buy expensive gas out of barrels or plastic jugs from locals, the quality of which is always questionable.

If you've got the time, there are numerous Tequila distilleries in this region. They are clearly marked off Mex 200. Some of the distilleries use hand made copper distilling pots, and the tequila is second to none. The local distillers are happy to let you taste the product because once you do, you'll likely buy some.

Colima is one of the smallest states in Mexico. It's a relatively prosperous state with a strong agricultural base fueling their economy. It's home to the powerful and unrelenting beach break of Pascuales, known by barrel riders worldwide. Aside from Pascuales there are a few other surfing options in Colima, however none are as fierce and heavy as Pascuales.

Colima receives most Pacific Ocean groundswell making it a good option during smaller swells and the offseason. The wind blows offshore here in the morning with uncanny predictability. The water is usually pleasant in the high 70's but can dip occasionally, especially in the fall and winter, so it's good to bring along a vest or even a spring suit for the coldest days.

If you're staying in Pascuales, be sure to check out the city of Tecoman. The people here have a unique hospitable charm and take pride in their clean and prosperous city. Tecoman is a great place to stock up on cheap goods and other supplies before you head down into Michoacán. Once you pass Tecoman there are not many places to stock up on supplies until you reach Lazaro Cardenas.

Edgar in the shaping room at Pascuales

Edgars Surf Camp is the best and most affordable place to stay in Pascuales. His English is perfect and he really does a great job of making everyone feel welcome. He knows the area and is willing to share a little local knowledge about other surfing options in the region. Aside from being a cool guy, Edgar is perhaps the best surfboard repair guy in all of Mexico. If you break a board at Pascuales (which you probably will) Edgar is your man. His work is top notch and he can usually finish most repairs in 24 hours for a very fair price.

Chamela

Just as Mex 200 begins to come down out of the mountains towards the coast you will come to the very small town of Chamela. There is a sign for the town and you will be able to see the ocean. There is a beach break here that has been known to hold some sand over the years, but surfing here is not very predictable. If you are in the area, it's worth a look, but Chamela is not a surf destination by most people's standards.

Barra De Navidad

About 10 km north of the Jalisco/Colima border you will see signs for Barra de Navidad. This is a neat little fishing village with a jetty/point setup that can make a decent wave. Barra de Navidad really needs a solid swell to turn on because it faces north. If there is a huge SW swell in the water, it can be worth checking out. Overall the vibe here is very mellow. If you go north a little bit towards the center of the bay, there can be some average beach break peaks worth checking out on smaller days.

La Boquita

Located at the north end of the Bahia Santiago about 15 km north of Manzanillo you'll find the right hand point setup of La

Boquita. Due to the orientation of this spot, it's usually small unless there is a massive SW swell running. If the conditions are right, you can find a fun and potentially long wave here on the right day. La Boquita is a very developed area and accommodations are more refined and expensive here, making it too costly to stay if you're working on a budget.

Olas Altas

About 4 km south from La Boquita is the beach break known as Olas Altas. Although it's protected also, the beach here is open to a bit more swell and usually is quite a bit larger than the point. There can be some fun sandbars here that work best on lower tides with the morning offshore winds.

La Termo

La Termo is situated at the outlet for the cooling towers at the local power plant, Planta Thermoelectrica Manuel Alverez. This break faces southwest and holds much more size. Because of the water being released from the plant, there can be epic sandbars here. It can also be closed out or blown out. If the wind is light and the swell is small to medium out of the south or southwest, it's worth checking out. Because of the cooling water being released at this break, the water is almost always warmer here. The backdrop is less than scenic with the smoke stacks right there, but the wave, at times, can make up for the lack of view.

Cuyutlan

About 20 km north of Tecoman you'll find the small beach town of Cuyutlan. There is an average beach break here that has its moments. It is usually worth checking out if the swell is smaller and the wind is down. It has been known to hold some good sandbars over the years but don't hold your breath.

Paraiso

To the north of Pascuales 5 km you'll find a more manageable beach break known as Paraiso. This break always seems to be about half the size and power of Pascuales. It works on a variety of tides and is almost always off shore in the morning. It's a good option if Pascuales is too heavy for your liking.

Pascuales

Ten kilometers west of Tecoman is the famed break, Boca de Pascuales. This world-class beach break will usually handle any size south swell the Pacific Ocean can dish out. Pascuales usually has a few different peaks working. During the summer months and on weekends the lineup can get crowded with highly competent local surfers. The vibe here is much more friendly and mellow than its rival wave, Puerto Escondido. Give respect to the locals and you will be welcomed warmly by a local crew that is more inviting to outsiders than you might expect.

Barrels in Pascuales- T. Schmidt

The wind will blow off shore nearly every morning and generally gets blown out by noon. An evening glass off isn't uncommon but don't expect it. Pascuales works on a variety of different tides and with constantly changing sand bars, no two waves are ever the same. Cavernous board-snapping barrels are the rule more than the exception. Pascuales is not a beginner wave and demands respect. Strong rips occur often requiring a heightened level of awareness. If you are unsure of your abilities don't go out; Pascuales is an unforgiving wave that has claimed a few lives over the years.

The best place to stay on a budget is Edgar's Surf Camp. When you get to Pascuales, it's the first place on the left when the road hooks to the right. Both the camping and the rooms are fairly priced. If Edgar's is booked up, there are a few other places along the beach that generally cost a bit more. Most of the locals have a cabana or two that they will happily rent if you ask around.

El Real

About 5 km south of Pascuales is El Real, another series of beach breaks that can get good and tend to be less heavy and crowded than Pascuales. This small beach strip is popular with local Mexicans for day trips to the beach. Not many surfers go to El Real, however at times there can be great sand bars here that are empty and rival Pascuales.

Boca de Apisa

About 35 km south of Tecoman look for the clearly marked sign to Boca de Apisa in the town of Cerro de Ortega. The river is right on the border of Michoacan and Colima. This spot works on most groundswells producing rights and lefts over fickle sandbars that can be epic or lousy. When it's working the waves here are high quality.

MICHOACAN

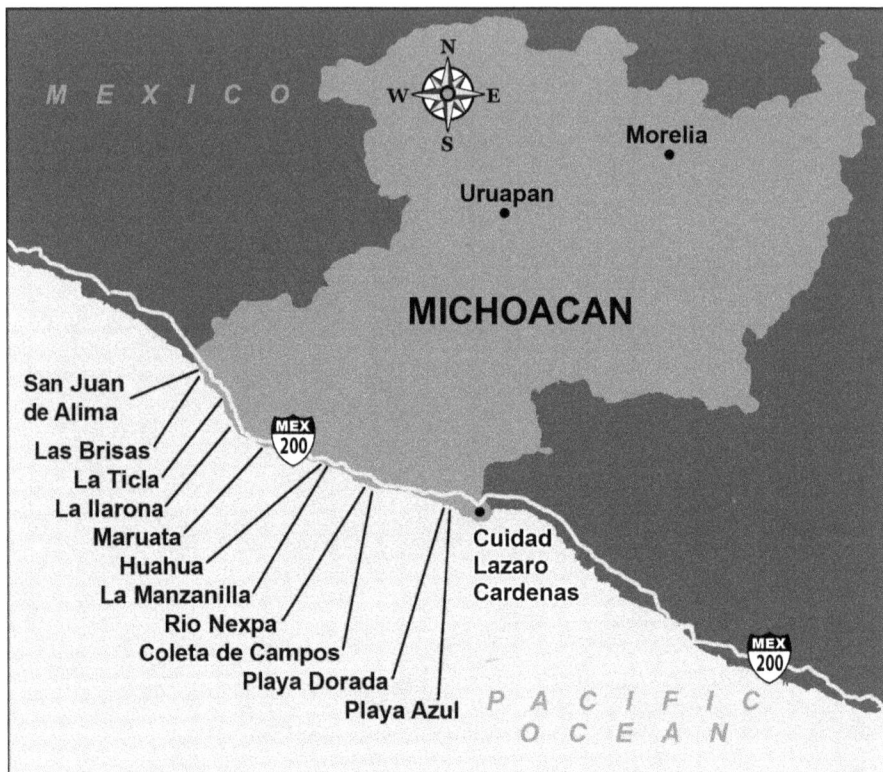

The rich and verdant coastline of Michoacan is home to some of Mexico's most promising surf destinations. Situated in the middle of the country, Michoacan is open to a wide swell window producing waves nearly year round. The coast is largely pristine and has managed to avoid the rampant development typical of many coastal regions in Mexico. With no major airports in coastal Michoacan, most of the tourist traffic is diverted elsewhere, leaving many of the beaches sparsely occupied by only those travelers with a high threshold for adventure.

The people in these coastal villages are friendly and welcoming to travelers because much of their subsistence is derived from the sparse tourism sector. The seafood here is world class with fresh fish caught and served every day. Accommodations are cheap, plentiful and extremely basic, catering to travelers who seek simplicity and affordability. If you're looking for four-star luxury resorts, Michoacan is not the place. The rustic atmosphere of coastal Michoacan is best suited for hardcore surfers with a no frills approach to travel.

If you're going to visit Michoacan, your best bet is to fly into Manzanillo or Zihautanejo. Either way, you're still going to be several hours from the heart of the surf scene. Mex 200 hugs the winding coast here making for a slow and exhausting drive through the tropical mountain landscape. The road is possibly the most dangerous in all of coastal Mexico with few pull offs, no guardrails, and overgrown plant life encroaching on the road. Exercise extreme caution and take your time when driving in Michoacan.

Rio Nexpa and La Ticla are the most popular spots in Michoacán, both consistently producing quality waves. Interspersed between these two main breaks you'll find a series of other noteworthy spots that tend to be far less crowded.

Michoacan is truly the wild west of Mexico. Police presence is minimal and the closest hospitals are hours away in either Lazaro Cardenas or Tecoman. If you stay in Michoacan, come prepared and use your best judgment. Most importantly, be ready to score some of the best waves of your life.

San Juan de Alima

About an hour south of Tecoman Mex 200 will cut right into the town of San Juan de Alima at km 209. It a picturesque beach with moderate surf potential. This beach is a good option in the winter, as it tends to pick up northwesterly swells better than most other beach breaks in the area. The town has a very mellow vibe with great seafood and cheap accommodations. The surf here is fickle but can pick up on occasion.

Las Brisas

After winding through the mountains south of San Juan de Alima you'll come to an epic vista point with a restaurant on the right at about km 203. The beach breaks you can see are Las

Brisas. These peaks are almost always empty and can get quite good on a lower incoming tide with smaller swells. Not many people surf here because of the proximity of so many quality waves. Las Brisas is a good option if La Ticla and Rio Nexpa aren't quite big enough to really be working.

La Ticla

At the mouth of the Rio Ostula you will find the famed cobblestone reef break known as La Ticla. It's about an hour and a half south of Tecoman off Mex 200 at km 183. There is a clearly marked sign at the beginning of the four km road that takes you down to the small village. This spot breaks year round on most groundswells. The winds blow predominantly off shore in the mornings creating semi-hollow peeling rights and lefts. La Ticla works on most tides if there is significant swell but shows its best form on a lower to mid-tide. On a mid to large south swell the left will begin to work creating a long ripable wave that wraps around the headland into the bay.

In the busy season expect a moderate to heavy crowd consisting of mostly traveling surfers with some locals too. The vibe here is mellow and respectful as the majority of the traveling surfers come together. You'll likely be hanging out with the same small pack of people in and out of the water. La Ticla is an excellent option when the waves are smaller or during wintertime north and west swells.

Accommodations are very affordable here with many options for camping, palapas and cabanas. There are a few small stores in town to buy basic goods and food, but it doesn't hurt to stock up on rations in Tecoman before you head down if you plan on being in La Ticla for a while. Depending on the waves you may be tempted to stay forever.

There have been some stories of robberies and violence in the Ticla area over the years, some of which are true. Keep track of your stuff as you would anywhere and be aware of your surroundings. Like the vast majority of the people who visit La Ticla, you should be fine.

La llarona

About 20 minutes south of Ticla at km 173, look for the signs to the small beach village of El Faro de Bucerias. This fickle right-hander works well on a small to medium south or west swell. When it's working, the swell refracts off the rocky headland to make a semi A-frame that can produce a rather heavy, but short barrel on the inside. It's usually less crowded than La Ticla or Nexpa, and at times can rival both of them in overall wave quality; La llarona is definitely worth a look.

Maruata

Thirty minutes south of La Ticla at km 149 is the small village of Maruata. The wave here is a protected, mellow right-hander that is suited more for beginners and long boarders. When the south swell is really cranking, it can have a bit more shape but is generally a mellow wave. This is a good option if it's too big or crowded at La Ticla. The crowd here is usually mellow, with mostly beginners/intermediate surfers and kids. Look for the signs on the Mex 200; it's clearly marked. Take the road into town and then go to the left. Once you're in town, go right towards the ocean and you'll find the spot. There are really cheap cabanas and camping here and some top quality seafood too.

Huahua

Located 30 kilometers north of Nexpa at km 85, Huahua is a prominent hip in the Michoacan coastline with a river running through the middle of it. There is a right on the south side and a left on the north side, both of which can produce long quality waves. Huahua likes a medium to solid south swell to really work. The dirt road that runs along the river often washes out, making it difficult to drive all the way to the beach; you may have to walk the last few hundred meters. You can also drive into the town, slightly to the south, and park at the end of the road; you'll see a small palapa where the road ends. Look to the north and you'll see the waves if they're breaking.

There is not much in Huahua and traveling surfers stick out in this quiet beach town. This area is a hotspot for marijuana farmers and other drug related activity, so keep your wits about you and watch your back. Huahua is worth checking out if the crowd at Nexpa is too overwhelming.

La Manzanilla

There is an average quality beach break here that is worth checking out on smaller glassy days. La Manzanilla seems to work best in the winter on smaller days especially on combo swells. The exit to this tiny little town is next to the bridge at about km 81. If you're looking for it, go slowly because it comes up out of nowhere on the winding road.

Rio Nexpa

At the clearly marked turnoff on Mex 200 at km 55 at Rio Nexpa you will find one of Mexico's longest left hand point breaks. This south swell magnet can produce some of the best lefts in North America. Nexpa likes a solid south and tends to get soft and sections off unless there's a pretty good swell running. If it's solid, be sure to walk all the way out to the headland and paddle through the breakers. If you try to paddle from the bay, you'll never make it and the incessant current will push you further to the north.

Endless lefts at Rio Nexpa

The paddle factor here can be significant so be ready for a workout. The 300-meter rides make it all worthwhile. You'll have ample time to practice drawn out roundhouse cutbacks over and over again. In the summer months Nexpa can get crowded, it's really a roll of the dice. Nexpa is very quiet and laid back with few distractions, making for a very relaxing surf destination. There's an internet café in town but it's very expensive. Keep in mind that there's a better and cheaper one a short drive to the south in Coleta de Campos.

There are plenty of options for camping and accommodations in Rio Nexpa, all of which are very affordable. When you arrive, ask around and find the best deal before you commit to anything. Be wary of places that have no other surfers staying there. There are two small *tiendas* in town with basic necessities. For a better selection of rations, go south a few minutes to Coleta de Campos and you'll find many more stores and supplies.

Carving into a clean wall at Coleta de Campos

Coleta de Campos

About 5 kilometers south of Nexpa at km 51 you'll come across the small village of Coleta de Campos. This quaint little town is home to some shops and restaurants situated on an idyllic crescent shaped bay. Hidden from view and unknown to all but the most savvy tourists, this place is largely off the map. On a medium or better south swell, the waves wrap around the breakwater at the north end of the bay creating a fun little lined up right hander that is usually uncrowded. A host of local groms dominate this spot but are usually accepting of polite visitors when it comes to sharing their wave. Coleta is a good option if Nexpa is blown out, or if you're tired of going left. There are also some good restaurants, supplies and a cheap internet cafe.

Playa Dorada

About 30 kilometers north of Lazaro Cardenas there's a series of beach breaks in the small village of Playa Dorada. The place caters to tourists more than the breaks to the north so the town can get a bit crowded. The waves are generally empty with most of the beachgoers sticking to the sand. On smaller days when the sand is right, you can find a little peak almost always to yourself. It works well in the winter on smaller fragmented swells on a lower tide. Playa Dorada can be fickle but always worth a check as its right off Mex 200 and guaranteed to be less crowded than Nexpa.

Playa Azul

At the intersection of Mex 200 and 37 you can head towards the coast to find the town of Playa Azul. There are some beach breaks here that can work on smaller swells. This is a quality beach break that is often overlooked and is worth checking out, especially if the swell is smaller and the winds are down.

GUERRERO

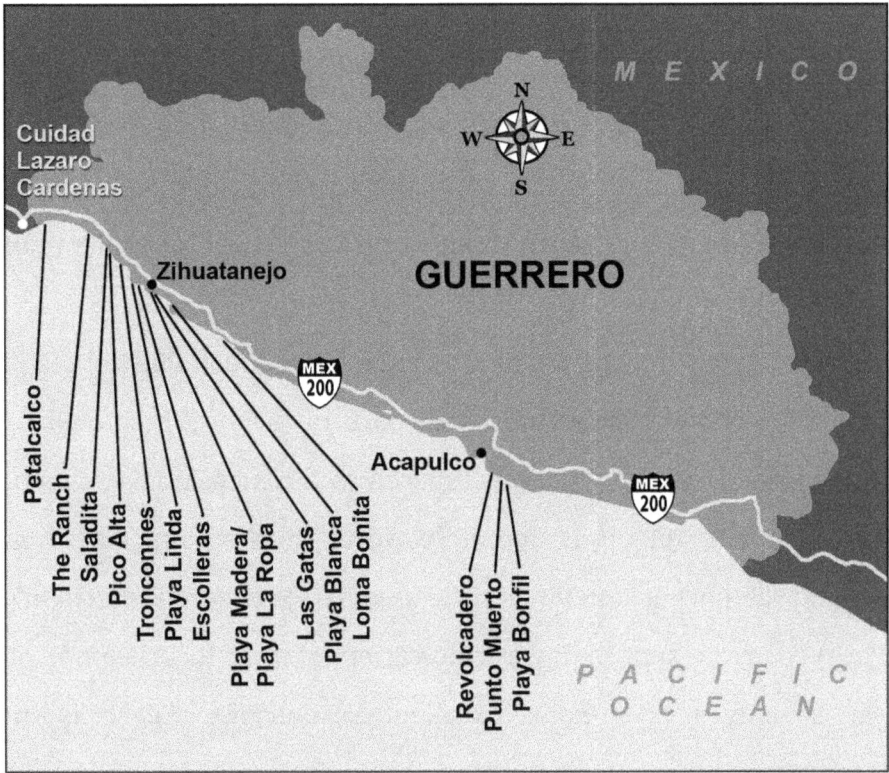

The Guerrero coastline is varied and expansive producing many different setups, some of which are among the best in Mexico. One of the poorer states in Mexico, much of Guerrero's economy relies on domestic and international tourism in Acapulco, Zihuatanejo and Ixtapa.

Acapulco is Guerrero's largest city with just under 1 million inhabitants. Driving through Acapulco is a stressful undertaking, especially during rush hour. The sea of traffic amplified by a total disregard for traffic laws and a never-ending supply of kamikaze taxi cab drivers will surely test your nerves. Be attentive while driving through Acapulco and look at the map before you enter. The good news is the view from the coastal bluffs provides an unparalleled vantage point. If there is traffic, you'll have plenty of time to take it all in.

The sleepy towns north of Zihuatanejo are home to many classic point and reef setups. The pace of life in Zihuatanejo is much more *tranquillo* when compared to the menacing streets of Acapulco. Zihuatanejo is definitely worth checking out. The area around the harbor known as the *Paseo del Pescador* (Fisherman's Path) is a great spot to buy a wide variety of fresh local seafood or eat at one of the many excellent restaurants. There is an interesting archeological museum at the south end of the *Paseo del Pescador* with artifacts from the Olmec, Toltec and Aztecs, giving a look into the rich and varied history of Guerrero. If you're looking for a break from surfing, Zihuatanejo is an affordable destination to spend a day or two exploring town. Just north of Zihautanejo is the tourist resort of Ixtapa. This government planned resort caters more to wealthy travelers seeking a predictable, insular travel experience. With that said, very few traveling surfers stay in Ixtapa.

Parts of Guerrero are still the Wild West. It's always prudent to keep your wits about you and remember that much of this state is very economically depressed. Many thousands of surfers visit Guerrero every year and have a wonderful time. There shouldn't be any reason you will too if you're reasonably cautious and aware of your surroundings.

Petalcalco

Just south of Lazaro Cardenas is the small beach town of Petalcalco. There's a river mouth here and an average beach break to the north. The town itself doesn't have much to offer and isn't an ideal camping location due to the lack of facilities. If you're looking for an uncrowded beach break on a smaller day, you'll likely find a wave here.

The Ranch

The ranch is a series of reefs on a very isolated stretch of coast that produces quality waves on any solid swell. This spot works best on southerly swells and can hold up to 15 feet. There are many different options here, but the left on the north end tends to provide the longest walls.

If you want to get to the ranch there are a few options. The easiest but most expensive is to hire a boat from Saladita to take you up there. If you can organize a group it will cut the cost down considerably. If you're unfamiliar with the area, it's advisable to go by boat with a knowledgeable local.

Lonely barrels at the Ranch

If you have a truck or 4x4, you can drive by heading north on Mex 200 from Zihuatanejo, at km 56 take a right (yes right) towards El Chico. Take your first left about 300 meters down the road once you turn off Mex 200. You will go over Mex 200 on an overpass. Follow the road for about 1 km and stay to the left when it splits into three roads. Follow that road for about 2 km and stay to the right when that road splits again. This road will take you all the way down to the break. This route will take you on isolated one-lane dirt roads that are very poorly maintained. If you are unsure of your rig or your comfort level, we strongly suggest hiring a boat. There are no services or stores if you drive. Come prepared with everything you will need for the day and park your rig within eyesight.

Saladita

Saladita is an extremely long left hand point that needs a sizeable south swell to really do its thing. When it's smaller, Saladita is still an excellent long board wave. It works best on a lower incoming tide. Offshore winds tend to prevail in the morning. Evening glass-off sessions are not uncommon either.

To get to Saladita head north from Zihautanejo to km marker 40 and take a left into the market town of Los Llanos. Drive through town and then take a right on the road marked for Saladita. If you get lost, ask someone in Los Llanos where Saladita is, they will point you in the right direction.

There are a few places to stay in Saladita. When you get into town, there are some *palapas* you can rent to the left in the palm grove. Accommodations in Saladita are surprisingly expensive considering how basic they are. If you're there in the off season, you may be able to work a deal but otherwise expect to pay upwards of 400 pesos/night for basic accommodations. Camping is also an option but you'll have to ask around. There are basic goods and food in Saladita, but if you're planning on staying for a while it's best to stock up on rations in Zihuatanejo.

Pico Alta

Pico Alta is a much more serious wave than Saladita. Access is by boat only. It's about a 15-minute ride south from Saladita. Ask the local surfers in Saladita and organize a crew to hire a boat down for the morning. This wave is more fickle but it can produce barreling A- Frames.

Tronconnes

Located at km 30 north of Zihuatanejo you'll find the resort town of Tronconnes. There is a decent beach break here that has been known to hold some excellent waves over the years. The wave works best on smaller swells and tends to close out on the larger days. There are many high-end boutique hotel/resorts here, and even in the off-season you can expect to pay upwards of 500 pesos/night for any room. Camping is sparse but available if you ask around.

Tronconnes Point

At the south end of the Tronconnes beach break is a large rocky point that produces long lefts that peel into the bay. For this spot to really work, it needs a solid south swell on a lower incoming tide. If it's good, you can expect a decent crowd but there are generally enough waves to go around for everyone.

Playa Linda

Just north of Club Med Ixtapa about 300 meters there is a breakwater. On the north end of the breakwater there is a mellow fun left that can produce long waves on the right swell. Isla Ixtapa shadows this spot so it's usually smaller than most breaks in the area.

Escolleras

To the south of the entrance to the Ixtapa Marina there is a powerful wedge like wave that is more suited for bodyboarders. It can be very heavy and dangerous. There are occasionally surfers out, but it's mostly a close out beach break refraction wave.

Playa Madera/Playa La Ropa

These are the two beaches fully within Zihuatanejo Bay. It's usually flat here unless there is a larger swell running. If there is, you can find waist to chest high beach break waves that tend to have good shape if the sand is built up, which it usually is.

Las Gatas

At the south end of Zihuatanejo Bay there is a point break that rarely fires. Las Gatas needs a really large southwest swell to turn on but when is does, it creates a quality left hand point producing long rides. If it's working, there will be a host of locals dominating. If you show respect you can get a few waves out here but expect a crowd.

Playa Blanca

If you follow the signs southward for Zihuatanejo Airport there is an average beach break spot adjacent to the airport. Playa Blanca is almost always uncrowded and definitely worth checking out on smaller days when the wind is down.

Loma Bonita

Loma Bonita is about 45 minutes south of Zihuatanejo. It's a very chilled out beach town that caters to surfers and backpackers who are looking for something off the beaten path. The sand bar setups here can be awesome, providing hollow dredging beach break peaks if the conditions are right. Overall the whole vibe here is very mellow. During the summer there are almost always waves at Loma Bonita.

Revolcadero

Just south of Acapulco Bay you will see signs for Playa Revolcadero. This is an average beach break set up that can hold some good waves. If it is working, you can expect it to be crowded since it's close to the city. If you are already in the area, be sure to check out Punto Muerto to the south. It tends to have a bit better shape.

Punto Muerto

If you follow the signs to Acapulco airport and then head towards the beach you'll find Punto Muerto. It's a beach break that can hold some solid swell and tends to have very good shape. Lots of A-Frame peaks are common. Because of the proximity to

Acapulco you should expect a crowd of mostly local Mexicans since not too many traveling surfers visit here.

Playa Bonfil early morning barrel

Playa Bonfil

This beach is directly parallel to Acapulco Airport. The sand here tends to set up very well, providing lined up rights and lefts. Playa Bonfil works best around head high, but can hold larger waves. There will almost always be other surfers here, but there are usually enough waves to go around. It's usually best to go early in the morning before the wind kicks up, however it's not uncommon for it to stay glassy all day. Accommodations are available, but most of the hotels are a bit pricey. If you are there in the off-season, you can usually get a deal on accommodations.

OAXACA

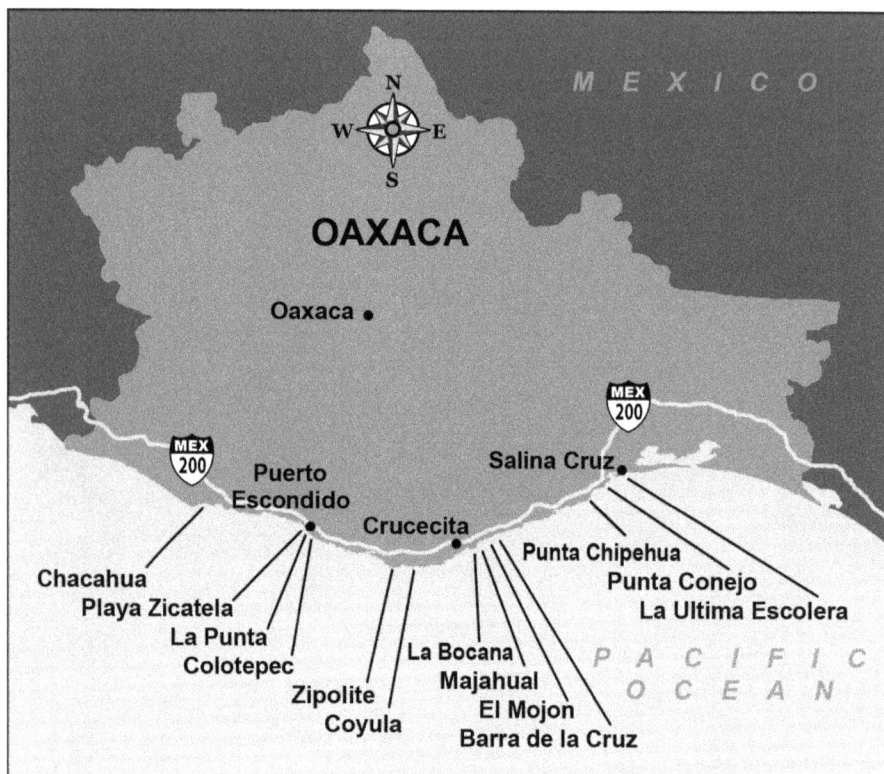

Oaxaca is the crown jewel of the Pacific Coast of Mexico. The beautiful coastline wraps and contorts endlessly, making it one of North America's last true surf frontiers. There are so many turns and twists in the stretch of coast south of Puerto Escondido, you would have to spend the rest of your life sailing the coast looking for these otherwise inaccessible points in order to surf it all.

Tourism is prevalent in Oaxaca making it generally safe and more predictable. As a result, there is never any shortage of international travelers all seeking to enjoy this unique and majestic coast. Puerto Escondido is the most well known spot among surfers seeking heavy punishing barrels. The town serves as an anchor point for traveling surfers; you'll tend to run into the same faces here if you spend any significant amount of time in Oaxaca.

Oaxaca is easily accessible by plane with airports in Puerto Escondido, Huatulco and Salina Cruz. There are many busses and collectivos that travel between these regions too, all of which are reasonably priced and run fairly often. If you're looking to get out of Puerto Escondido to surf elsewhere, ask around. There are always people headed out to surf other breaks who will be happy to share the gas bill with you.

The Mex 200 is very curvy in Oaxaca but the road surface is generally in better shape than some stretches in Michoacan and Guererro. There are many military checkpoints in Oaxaca, so always keep your pertinent documents on hand for inspection. When traveling south of Puerto Escondido, be sure to stock up on supplies in town before you leave as there isn't much once you get south of Huatulco. Your best bet is visiting the Super Che (Supermarket) in either Puerto Escondido or Huatulco. Both have a great selection of reasonably priced food if you're traveling on a limited budget.

Chacahua

The wave in Chacahua is world class when there's a good south swell and the sand is right. When everything comes together, you'll find a peeling right-hander that is capable of producing multiple barrel sections. Most people only surf it on an incoming tide as the pull from the outgoing tide can make it impossible to stay in position. The easiest way to get out is to walk to the end of the breakwater and climb down the rocks, then paddle over to the take off zone.

Chacahua perfection

There are two ways to get to Chacahua and for most people we advise taking the boat from Zapotolita. If you want to drive to Chacahua take your 4x4 and nerves of steel north about 20 kilometers to the town of San Juan Del Progresso and then head towards the ocean following the signs to Galera. It's a long, sketchy drive and it is doable. You will need a good map and the ability to speak at least some Spanish.

To get a boat, drive to Zapotolita about 45 minutes north of Puerto Escondido. At km 82 you'll see a sign for the town of Zapotolita. Follow the road as it hooks to the left along the shore of the Chacahua lagoon. Local kids will try to flag you down to take their boat but it's usually too expensive. Continue a few more streets until you see the fenced in parking lot on the right with a small dock out front. It's a good indication if there are other surfers' cars parked there. We have left our cars for weeks on end in this parking lot with no problems, but it's still advisable to bring all your valuables with you.

You'll have to negotiate a price for a boat ride out there. Don't pay more than 250 pesos per boat or 50-60 pesos per person for a ride to the Chacahua. Make sure you are going all the way to the village and not across the lagoon to the collectivo that drives you along the beach to Chacahua. You can do this but it's a long ride on the collectivo and ends up costing about the same anyway. The boat ride through the mangroves in the lagoon is worth the experience.

Once you're there, you'll find different choices for accommodations. Most of the local restaurant owners have rooms for rent in the 100-250 peso range. There are also camping options, just ask around. Keep in mind when staying in Chacahua that you are in an isolated village only accessible by boat, so plan accordingly. There are a few small stores to buy beer and other necessities but it's best to bring food with you from Puerto Escondido if you want to eat cheaply.

Puerto Escondido

Puerto Escondido is a medium sized town that's home to two breaks, Playa Zicatela and La Punta. The name Puerto Escondido is often used to refer to the beach break, which is actually known as Playa Zicatela. Besides world-class waves, the town has a lot to offer the traveling surfer. There are always plenty of travelers from all corners of the globe enjoying this town's lively vibe. There's a healthy mix of surfers and non surfers, guys and girls, Mexicans, Europeans, Australians and North Americans here making for a nice change of pace if you've been camped out at Chacahua for too long. The nightlife here is fun and often carries into the morning, making Puerto Escondido an excellent spot to party.

Puerto Escondido has grown immensely over the past 20 years but still retains its small town charm. You won't find high-rise hotels and other monstrosities here. Puerto Escondido has done a great job of managing growth without spoiling the charm that people come for year after year.

Accommodations in Puerto Escondido vary from basic to luxury. If you're looking for bare bones, there are a few hostels that are dirt cheap and pretty grungy overall. If you want something a step up, Hotel Acaurio is one of our favorites. It's beach front and centrally located next to the OXXO (convenient store) on the main strip. The place is clean, cheap, has a pool and they will generally cut you a good deal if you want to stay for a week or more. If you're looking to really kick back and enjoy a more luxurious stay, we suggest Casa de Dan and Carmen. This well-designed hotel compound is located above all the noise from the strip with an epic view of Playa Zicatela. If you want to relax in a Shangri-La like environment, and you have the extra cash, check out Dan and Carmen's, where many of the traveling pros stay.

Playa Zicatela

This world-class beach break is called the Mexican Pipeline for a reason. If there is any south swell, you'll know it at Playa Zicatela as this stretch of beach channels in any south swell. The wind tends to blow offshore in the morning and usually holds until about noon then comes onshore. It's not uncommon for it to glass off in the afternoon though.

A manageable day at Playa Zicatela, Puerto Escondido

There are a variety of peaks here, rights and lefts, all of which are heavy. Zicatela will hold just about any size swell. It tends to be crowded when it's smaller but once it starts pushing double overhead the pack thins out substantially as the men and women are separated from the boys and girls. If you are unsure of your ability, don't go out. People have drowned here on more than one occasion.

The local crew here is a bit more aggressive toward outsiders than most places in Mexico. Don't expect to make friends with the locals. They deal with a constant rotation of traveling surfers year round and don't give waves to anyone they don't know. Give respect where it's due, wait your turn, don't snake anyone and you should have no problems at Playa Zicatela.

La Punta

At the south end of Playa Zicatela is the long left hand point known simply as La Punta. The lefts will start to work when there is a significant south swell in the water. If Playa Zicatela is under head-high don't expect much at La Punta. If it's good, it's almost always crowded. Look out for rocks on the lower tide - you'll see the boils in the faces of the waves.

Colotepec

About 20 minutes south of Puerto Escondido at the mouth of the Colotepec River there is a decent beach break that can hold sandbars that rival the quality of Zicatela. The wave here is much less crowded than Zicatela. If you have a car, it's definitely worth checking out. Go early in the morning and you will likely find it empty with light offshore winds that usually hold up until about noon.

Zipolite

There is a beach break here of average quality that usually holds a decent wave. The town of Zipolite is a haven for artists, hippy expatriates and backpackers. Aside from surfing, Zipolite is worth checking out if you're surfed out or just need a change of scenery for a few days. The rugged coastline provides excellent snorkeling and spear fishing opportunities too. Cheap accommodations are abundant with camping and cabanas available.

Coyula

About 15 km south from Puerto Angel on Mex 200 you will see a road at the *Puente Coyula*, (Coyula Bridge). Follow this road to the small town at the beach. There is a rocky headland at the river mouth that deposits a sandbar. There has been a quality right hand point off and on over the years here. There is not much in the sleepy town of Coyula so come prepared with everything you will need before you get there. If the swell is too small, the point will likely not work, but south down the beach a little ways there is a decent beach break that tends to work. Coyula is great if you're looking to explore a bit and avoid the crowds at Barra and Puerto.

La Bocana

At the southern end of the city of Huatulco look for the sign to La Bocana. There is an average beach break here that works best on a lower incoming tide and is almost never crowded but doesn't do great on a south swell. In the wintertime on more northwesterly swells and local wind swells this stretch of beach break can light up providing punchy A-frame peaks.

El Mojon

At km 171, 5 kilometers north of Barra De La Cruz, you'll see a small poorly maintained dirt road that takes you down about 2 kilometers to the lesser-known point break of Mojon. This right hand point is more fickle than Barra de la Cruz but can produce reeling barrels that rival most other points in the region. It works best on smaller south swells with a lower tide. El Mojon can close out with too much size, but is an excellent option if you're tired of the crowd at Barra on the smaller days. Pack your lunch because there is nothing here but a few houses and usually just a few, or no surfers out. Tread lightly at this spot and don't advertise if it's good. Most people will just stay at Barra if they don't know about it, and many do not.

Majahual

If you hike over the small hill to the north from Mojon, there is another point/ river mouth setup known as Majahual. You can see it from atop the hill. This place totally depends on the sand deposits from the river mouth but over the years has produced some epic right hand barrels. This place is totally remote and if it's been working the locals may not be happy to see you. If you're already at Mojon its worth checking out. Be extremely careful when hiking over the hill from Mojon because the dirt is loose and there's cactus everywhere.

Early morning session at Barra de la Cruz

Barra de la Cruz

At km 176 you'll see the signs for the small village of Barra de la Cruz. Follow the road into town past the soccer fields and then turn to the right. There are a few options for accommodations in Barra, all of which are basic and cheap. Pepe's Cabana's is centrally located and one of our favorites. Pepe is an awesome guy, generous, honest and probably one of the mellowest surf camp owners out there. His rates vary depending on the time of the year, but they are always fair. If Pepe's is booked up, look around. There are a lot of other options for accommodations in Barra.

The wave is world class. It needs a medium south swell to start really turning on and tends to like the lower tides. It's a sand bottom right hand point that can easily produce 200 + meter rides when it's on. The crowds can get insane, but if it's on there are generally enough waves for most competent surfers. The vibe tends to be mellow. Locals will demonstrate their priority, but they are welcoming to those who show respect and wait their turn. Don't make enemies here. It's very isolated and the locals all know each other and don't care if you're some big shot at your home break, or on the ASP.

In recent years the townspeople began charging 20 pesos/day to access the beach. There's only one road in, so there's really is no getting around it. There's a gate on the road and it's 20 pesos whether you're on foot or in a car. A lot of surfers gripe about it, but once you get six roundhouse cutbacks and a barrel or two per wave, you'll forget about the nominal fee.

The Salina Cruz Region Overview

Salina Cruz is home to isolated, amazing right hand point breaks. The opportunity for discovery is still huge in this region. The points listed in this section are not secrets, however they aren't widely known either. If you go to these listed spots other surfing opportunities will present themselves. This region is littered with right hand points. It is not our intention to spoil the thrill of discovery. If you search around in the region north of Salina Cruz you will be rewarded with quality point breaks. We simply can't give away all the secrets.

Salina Cruz is plagued by howling winds that start around mid October and last through March. If you're planning on scoring during this time, you may be disappointed as the wind rarely cooperates. If you are there in the summer months, however, you can expect relatively clean conditions with morning offshore wind almost everyday.

Punta Chipehua

About 30 kilometers north of Salina Cruz is another long sand bottom point called Punta Chipehua. This long point has different sections and depending on the sand set up, it can produce lengthy rides. Chipehua tends to be far less crowded than Barra de la Cruz, but more fickle too.

To access Punta Chipehua take Mex 200 to the small town of Majada Villalobos and head towards the point. There is only one road out to the point and it's pretty obvious. There isn't much in the town so bring supplies with you. Camping is possible here. Talk to the local landowners and they will likely let you camp for a nominal fee.

Punta Conejo

About 10 kilometers north of Salina Cruz is Punta Conejo. This classic right hand point break rivals all other points in the area creating long, walled up waves, often with makeable barreling sections. The crowd here is usually mellow. There are a few surf camps in the area that have been known to act like they own the breaks. If you show respect and don't bring a huge crowd, they probably won't give you any trouble.

To access Punta Conejo, head towards the beach off Mex 200 at the intersection of Mex 200 and the road that head to Santa

Domingo Tehuantepec. The salt mines should be to the south of you at this point. Head about 3 km out that road and you will be able to see the ocean and the point. Don't leave any valuables in your car. If you have a 4x4 you can just drive right out onto the beach.

La Ultima Escolera (The Last Jetty)

To the south of the harbor in Salina Cruz there is a large crescent shaped jetty that feeds into a sand beach. This spot can produce a fast, barreling A-frame on smaller south swells. It works best on a lower incoming tide. If the swell is small and the points aren't really working check out la ultima escollera.

www.ingramcontent.com/pod-product-compliance
Lightning Source LLC
Chambersburg PA
CBHW060807110426
42739CB00032BA/3135